LOVING GOD

WITH ALL MY
MIND

His love is written all across the sky . . .

Jon Mohr / Michael W. Smith

Julie Ackerman Link

Discovery House Publishers is affiliated with RBC Ministries,
Grand Rapids, MI 49501.

Requests for permission to quote from this book should be directed to:
Permissions Department, Discovery House Publishers, P.O. Box 3566,
Grand Rapids, MI 49501.

Also available in the Loving God Series:

For more information visit Discovery House Publishers on the Web:
http://www.dhp.org/

Scripture quotations are taken from the Holy Bible, New International
Version®. © 1973, 1978, 1984 by International Bible Society. Used by
permission of Zondervan Publishing House. All rights reserved.

Part of the section titled "Believing in God's Son" is adapted from the
introduction, written by Julie Ackerman Link, to *Faith: A Holy Walk*, ©
1999 by the Oswald Chambers Publications Association, Ltd. Used by
permission of Discovery House Publishers, Grand Rapids, MI 49501.

Cover Photo: Corbis

Printed in the United States of America

06 07 08 09 10 11 12 / JRC / 10 9 8 7 6 5 4 3 2 1

Introduction

Why can't everyone just get along? We all say we want peace, so why is there so much conflict?

Well, the simplistic answer is because we can't agree about such basic things as right and wrong, good and bad, just and unjust.

If these conflicts were just between unbelievers we could understand. But Christians battle one another as well. Since we all claim to worship the same God—the one true God—our disagreements raise the question of whether we are really worshiping God or our individual ideas and perceptions of Him. Despite Scripture and centuries of Christian history to teach us, we have many of the same disputes as the early church.

Little has been written as to why Jesus added "mind" to the Greatest Commandment (Mark 12:30), but the apostle Paul gave a clue in his first letter to the church in Corinth. Much of the New Testament was addressed to a Gentile audience, primarily those influenced by the Greeks. In contrast to the Jews who were looking for signs, the Greeks were looking for wisdom (1 Corinthians 1:20-25). To them, the *mind* was the center of life.

As the seeds of the gospel were sown outside the land of Israel, some began growing in thorny places where paganism, with its many gods and goddesses, had long been the prevailing belief. In the city of Colossae, located in what is now modern day Turkey, new Christians were stumbling over their pagan roots. They wanted to add Jesus to their list of deities rather than honor Him as God. They wanted to keep their religious practices which gave "the appearance of wisdom with . . . their harsh treatment of the body" (Colossians 2:23). Paul responded to such heresies with these words: "Set your minds on things above, not on earthly things" (3:2).

In a letter written about the same time to another church, Paul pleaded with two women living in Philippi "to agree with each other in the Lord." He urged others in the congregation to help them, and in this case he actually told the people what to think:

> [W]hatever is true, whatever is noble, whatever is right, whatever is pure, whatever is lovely, whatever is admirable—if anything is excellent or praiseworthy—think about such things. . . . And the God of peace will be with you.
>
> —Philippians 4:8-9

If followed, this "mental antidote" for disagreement does indeed lead to peace. Imagine how blissful life would

The mind controlled by the Spirit is life and peace.

Romans 8:6

be if everyone in your family, church, workplace, or circle of friends thought only about things that are excellent and praiseworthy.

The temptation is to immediately imagine a world in which everyone agrees with our own definitions of these two words. But the "formula" only works when everyone agrees with God's definition.

> [D]o not let yourselves be conformed to the standards of this world. Instead, keep letting yourselves be transformed by the renewing of your minds; so that you will know what God wants and will agree that what he wants is good, satisfying and able to succeed.
>
> —Romans 12:2 *The Complete Jewish Bible*

Imagine! Created beings not only can *know* the mind of the Creator, we can *know* that what He wants for us is good, satisfying, and able to succeed.

Agreeing with God

One near-death experience was all it took to make me change my driving habits forever. It started with an ordinary bike ride. I hopped on my ten-speed and headed down a busy two-lane street with a 55-mph speed limit.

Partway to my destination, I hit a stone in the road, lost control of my bike, and went hurtling head-long across the pavement. Just then a car went whizzing past. If the driver had been passing me as most drivers do—without moving into the passing lane—I would have been road-kill. But he went around me as if passing a car—and by doing so he spared my life.

Like I said, the experience changed the way I drive. It also made me passionate about changing the way others drive—particularly my husband.

Jay has made much improvement over the years. On

our way to visit friends recently, he steered the car all the way into the left lane to pass a person on a bicycle. "Did you notice how I passed that kid on the bike?" he asked. "I did it because I know it makes you happy."

As soon as the words were out of his mouth, I realized that my strategy to protect bike riders had failed. If he does it only to please me, he probably does it only when I'm in the car. I want more than that from Jay. I want him to agree that my way of passing bikers is the best way to drive, not just my own paranoid personal preference.

For years I believed that the highest motive for doing good is the desire to please God. But when Jay's desire to please me left me unsatisfied, I began to doubt whether my own feeble desire to please God was satisfying to Him.

Yes, God wants me to obey because I want to please Him. But He also wants me to obey because I agree with

Him about what is right and good. He wants my mind as well as my heart to be aligned with His.

People often say that the three words they most love to hear are "I love you." Running a close second must be the words "You are right." I know parents who long to hear those words from their children, which makes me think that God longs to hear those same words from each of us.

The word *righteous* has been relegated to the dusty dictionaries of theologians. But being righteous is a way of saying to God, "You are right." The word is derived from the Old English words *right* and *wise,* and it means to act "in accord with divine or moral law; [to be] free from guilt or sin" (Merriam-Webster).

No offense, Merriam, but to act in accord with *moral*
law will not make anyone free from guilt or sin.
It will only make us *self*-righteous, which is
the condition that Jesus so vehemently
opposed, and which might also be the
unforgivable sin because those who are
self-righteous have no reason to think they
need the righteousness of Christ.

The word *righteous* in the New
Testament is the English translation of the
Greek word *dikaios*, which refers to "the
person whose way of thinking, feeling, and
acting is wholly conformed to the will of God."
Before any of us can be truly righteous, we must
acknowledge that it is God's right, not ours, to determine
what is right. Our part is to learn what God says is right

The ways of the LORD
are right; the righteous walk
in them, but the rebellious
stumble in them.

Hosea 14:9

and then to submit our minds to His transforming work until we agree with Him about what it is.

Agreeing with God about What Is Good

When I am being honest, I define "good" as whatever pleases me. I often use phrases like "That looks good . . . sounds good . . . smells good . . . tastes good . . . or feels good."

Now God is not opposed to pleasure. In fact, His first formal worship setting made provision for the enjoyment of all five of our senses. We call the structure a tabernacle, but it was really a tent—a very elaborate tent! It housed an ornate, gold-covered ark which held the stone tablets God gave to Moses on Mt. Sinai (God is not against beauty). It had an altar of incense where priests were to burn a blend of fragrant spices made by a perfumer

(God approves of pleasant aromas). It had an elaborate table with plates and pitchers (God appreciates a well-appointed dining experience). Around the tabernacle were curtains made from colorful yarn and finely twisted linen (God appreciates color and texture). Music was a component of worship as well, as we learn from reading 2 Chronicles 29:28 (God enjoys pleasing sounds).

Yes, God values what looks, sounds, smells, tastes, and feels good, and He wants us to enjoy these things. But He does *not* want us to worship them; He wants our enjoyment to remind us to worship Him, the creator and giver of all good things. If we think of our senses as being purely for pleasure, we'll eventually think that whatever brings us pleasure is good, and that's bad!

Look instead at this partial list of what the Bible says is good:

- It is good to be near God (Psalm 73:28).

- It is good to praise the Lord and make music to His name (Psalm 92:1).

- It is good to make requests, prayers, intercession, and thanksgiving for everyone—including kings and all those in authority—that we may live peaceful and quiet lives in all godliness and holiness (1 Timothy 2:1-4).

- It is good for our hearts to be strengthened by grace, not by ceremonial foods (or other rituals) (Hebrews 13:9).

Goodness is *not* what pleases us; it's what pleases God. And when our minds are aligned with God we'll choose things that please Him, which eventually will bring pleasure to us as well.

An amazing young woman from my church believes

with all her heart that "It is good to praise the Lord" (Psalm 92:1), and she is determined to do so despite how she feels. Jill and her husband, Darren, have suffered more tragedy in four years than most of us will experience in a lifetime. Three of their children, all in infancy, died of a rare genetic disorder. Less than a year after the death of their third baby, Jill was diagnosed with breast cancer, requiring aggressive treatment. But the darker her circumstances, the brighter her witness. Her online journal overflows with hope and praise, and through it she is a testimony of God's faithfulness even when He leads through the valley of the shadow of death. Jill recently wrote:

> The Lord has given to us and He has taken from us and through it we have to choose to continue to praise Him. It's certainly not easy to stand in front of your child's coffin and say, "Yes, Lord, I praise

you." It's not; it's impossible. But that's where He comes in. He doesn't leave you alone to suffer. He offers to walk beside—to give hope to the hopeless and peace where there is no peace to be found. He alone gives us the ability to praise Him when He asks us to walk through the longest desert. The first day that I got chemo I sat in the chair looking at that tube going into my port, unbelieving that this body was really mine, unbelieving that I was receiving chemotherapy. Then the song "Blessed Be Your Name" by Matt and Beth Redman came on my player. The questions and the grief came in waves as the medicine flowed in. How could I continue to praise Him? How long would we be required to walk the road marked with suffering? How, Lord? How? How long could we go on like

this? How long, Lord? I listened over and over.
Throughout these last couple years I've doubted.
I've questioned. I've wondered at His plan and
thought for sure that mine was better. But when it
comes down to it I know it's a choice. A choice to
praise Him even when life seems like it's just one
terrible thing after another, a choice to praise Him
when things are going so well that it seems like
we don't even need Him. It's a choice—a choice
with eternal consequences. A choice that is life-
changing—not only for yourself but also for those
around you.

Jill is following the pattern established by ancient Israel's
most famous songwriter. Even the darkest of David's songs
contains praise, not because his circumstances were great
but because he knew God was good.

Agreeing with God about What Is Satisfying

Early in my editorial career I worked on a book by Gary Smalley titled *Joy that Lasts*. The book was based on the metaphor of a cup. Gary's premise was that his dissatisfaction in life was the result of "filling his cup" with all the wrong things, though not necessarily bad things. He realized that he had been trying to find satisfaction in people, places, positions, and possessions. When he stopped expecting those things to provide fulfillment and began looking to God instead, he finally found satisfaction in his relationship with the Lord.

In contrast to what many people think they need to be satisfied—a spouse, children, love, understanding, acceptance, health, money, success, respect, approval, sex, revenge, vindication, more time, a better job—this is what the Bible says about satisfaction:

- If we delight in the Lord, He will satisfy our desires (Psalm 37:4).
- God's unfailing love is satisfying (Psalm 90:14).
- God satisfies every living thing (Psalm 145:16).
- God invites all who are thirsty and poor to come to Him and He will satisfy them with all that is good (Isaiah 55:1-2).
- If we spend ourselves on behalf of the hungry and satisfy the needs of the oppressed, . . . the Lord will guide us and satisfy our needs even in dry places (Isaiah 58:9-11).

Being a Christian involves more than accepting the claims of Christ because we like the idea of having Him pay for our sins so we can be spared the consequences. Christianity is a way of life that invites God to transform our thinking until we realize that everything He wants for us is good.

The cup metaphor showed me that obedience is not futilely struggling to empty my life of all that's bad; it's gladly filling it with everything God says is good. God doesn't want to drain pleasure out of life; He wants to fill life with purpose and meaning that enhance pleasure.

After the apostle Paul told the people of Colossae to set their minds on things above, not on earthly things (3:2), he seemed to do the exact opposite by bringing to mind a whole list of earthly things that they were to rid themselves of (v. 8). However, the very next paragraph suggests that the way to rid ourselves of earthly things is to fill our minds with heavenly thoughts—compassion, kindness, humility, gentleness, patience (v. 12), forgiveness (v. 13), love (v. 14), peace and gratitude (v. 15). The "secret" to doing this is tucked in the center of the paragraph: "Let the word of Christ dwell in you richly as you teach and admonish one another with all wisdom, and as you sing psalms, hymns and spiritual songs with gratitude in your hearts to God" (v. 16).

Simply put, when the singing and teaching of God's Word flows through our lives, all fears and doubts and evil thoughts and desires are washed away in the current.

AGREEING WITH GOD ABOUT WHAT IS SUCCESSFUL

My idea of success is to receive positive recognition for something I've done. But here again God's idea is different. Scripture has this to say about success:

- Anything done in disobedience to God cannot succeed (Numbers 14:41).

- Success comes only after obedience (Joshua 1:6-9).

- David had success because God was with him (1 Samuel 18:13-16).

- Nothing succeeds against the Lord (Proverbs 21:30).
- All "earthly" success is temporary and doomed to ultimate failure once God's plans have been accomplished (Daniel 11:36).

Even though words are "my business," I have not always used them well, or even honestly. The place where I first recall using words dishonestly was, sadly, in an Old Testament Bible Survey class. During each class period the professor would pass around a clipboard with every student's name on it. At the top of the page was one question: *Did you read the assignment?* We had to place a check mark beside our name in one of two columns: "yes" or "no." If we checked "yes," we got an A for the day. If we checked "no," we failed. It was that simple.

But here again, *simple* is the wrong word. To read the

entire Old Testament in one semester was no simple task. I didn't want to settle for anything less than an A, however, so I made sure I read every word. To make the assignment easier, I made up my own definition of the word *read*. I decided that it meant "to focus my eyes on a word." So that's what I did. I consciously looked at every word in every verse of the assigned reading.

Using my definition, I could speed through the assignment while carrying on a number of other tasks. And best of all, I could keep my conscience clear. But a clear conscience is not proof of right behavior (1 Corinthians 4:4).

When making the assignment the professor had more in mind than merely looking at words. He intended that I would convert the words from information into knowledge as they moved from my eyeballs to my mind.

And God's goal for the reading of His Word is even

more lofty. When the words of Scripture settle into our brains as knowledge, He desires that we recognize this knowledge as truth; that this truth will then flow from head to heart and be converted into love; and that love will then seep into every area of our lives, eventually finding its way into other lives as we go about living and breathing the beauty and truth of God's Word.

In my misguided attempt to keep up my grade point average, I was failing in something much more important: truthfulness. I also was missing the opportunity to become something much better than a good student; I was failing to become a godly person.

People today operate with much the same mindset that guided me as a college

"He defended the cause of the poor and needy, and so all went well. Is that not what it means to know me?" declares the LORD.

Jeremiah 22:16

freshman: we define truth in a way that enables us to succeed in whatever goal we have set. Some even argue that telling partial truths isn't bad as long as we do it for a good reason (for example, to get something done with fewer hassles) and it doesn't hurt anyone. But any success attained dishonestly does not fit God's definition of the word.

Remembering What God Has Done

Throughout Scripture God emphasizes the importance of remembering, and He encourages the use of memory devices. One of the first examples is found in the first book of the Bible. God placed a rainbow in the sky to remind Himself of His promise to never again destroy all life with a flood (Genesis 9:13-16).

Many years later when Moses addressed six hundred

thousand recently freed slaves and their families, he told the people to use memory devices to help them remember the commandments God had given to them:

> Tie them as symbols on your hands and bind them
> on your foreheads. Write them on the doorframes
> of your houses and on your gates.
>
> —Deuteronomy 6:8-9

God told the Israelites to remember such things as: The Sabbath (Exodus 20:8); The things you have seen (i.e., what God has done) (Deuteronomy 4:9); That God brought them out of slavery (Deuteronomy 5:15); The Lord, His laws, His decrees (Deuteronomy 8:11); That God is God and there is no other (Isaiah 46:9).

To help the people remember, God established an assortment of holiday celebrations during which the people were to stop working and take time to remember and enjoy everything God had done for them (see Leviticus 23).

All religious holidays are in fact memory devices. Christians have a set of holidays to remember the life and work of Christ.

Although the church I attend does not follow the liturgical calendar, last year I decided to participate in Lent, the forty-day-period when Christians remember Christ's great sacrifice for us by making a small sacrifice of our own.

To avoid having frequent reminders of my failure, I gave up something that isn't a big temptation for me: chocolate. Making this small sacrifice didn't make me more spiritual, but it did make me think differently. Fasting does not prove my goodness; it convinces me of God's, for it causes me to remember that God is the provider of all good things. Even my failure to fast successfully isn't bad because it reminds me that no one is good except God alone (Mark 10:18).

Like holidays, Scripture itself is a memory device. The stories of the Bible remind us of God's work in the past to redeem creation. Our own stories, or testimonies, remind us of the work God is doing today.

A few years ago my mom completed a project that I had been pestering her to do for years: she finished writing "part one" of her life story.

Over the years Mom had come up with many reasons for not doing this. Her best excuse was her fear that remembering would bring back too many painful memories. This was difficult for me to refute because it would be wildly selfish of me to say, "Do it anyway because I want to know my family history."

Eventually I encouraged her to think of it another way. "Do you think that after all these years you might have a different perspective on some of the things that happened?" I asked. "Maybe writing about them will actually make them less painful." The thoughtful look on her face encouraged me to continue. "Getting them out of your mind and onto paper might even be therapeutic."

Shortly after that she started writing, and little by little her story took shape. When it was finished, we chose pictures to include and had it printed. We then gave copies to family members at a special reunion.

Writing our life stories, and telling others about our spiritual journeys, is a way to remember and proclaim God's faithfulness: "I will sing of the LORD's great love forever; with my mouth I will make your faithfulness known through all generations" (Psalm 89:1).

Although each child must come to personal faith in Christ, it's important for believing parents and grandparents to communicate the story of their own spiritual pilgrimage (see Deuteronomy 6).

We are creating the memories for the next generation. Will they remember how we defended ourselves and our way of life or how we defended the poor and needy? Will they remember our attitudes of hate and vindictiveness or our words of love and compassion? Will they remember the stories we tell about the unfaithfulness of humans or the faithfulness of God? Will they wonder why we believe or know why we do?

Knowing Who God Is

Living out of a suitcase requires a skill that I lack: organization. So whenever I travel, I put my limited abilities into high gear. On one trip however my best efforts failed.

After getting out of the shower on our last morning in the hotel, I couldn't find my clean clothes. I searched for several minutes before asking Jay if he knew what had happened to them.

"Were they in a plastic bag?" he asked.

"Yes," I answered.

"Well, there were two plastic bags with clothes in them," he announced, as if the information would be news to me.

"I know," I said, "So where are they now?"

"I combined them."

"Why would you do that?" I moaned.

"I was just trying to help you get organized."

"But I *was* organized. The white bag was for clean and the brown one was for dirty."

"I'm sorry. I didn't know," he apologized. "They all looked the same."

"Where are they now?" I asked.

"I put them all together with my dirty clothes."

After going through a week's worth of dirty laundry I found some that seemed clean. By the time I finished getting dressed I had returned to a state of low-level civility.

When Jay sensed that it was safe to speak again, he said, "I don't want this story turning up in 'Our Daily Bread.'"

The thought didn't occur to me until he mentioned it (besides, the story was too long), but a possible application came quickly to mind. The book of Leviticus says, "You must distinguish between the holy and the common, between the unclean and the clean" (10:10).

In a world still swirling in sin thousands of years after its catastrophic collision with evil, the need for discernment is critical, and God has assigned to His followers the task of knowing the difference between good and evil. What separates God's people from everyone else is the wisdom He gives that enables them to discern holy from common, sacred from profane, clean from unclean, good from evil.

Shortly after we got back to Michigan, I had to be gone one afternoon. When I got home I discovered that Maggie, our dog, had "buried" some of my dirty clothes under Jay's pillow.

Maggie has learned to discern clean from unclean. Unfortunately, she prefers unclean. Old smelly clothes are as comforting to her as some of my old dirty sins are to me. But humans can learn that true discernment—the kind that God was trying to teach the children of Israel and that He wants all of His children to know—requires more than physical senses; it requires a relationship with the One who created us and who knows what is good for us.

Some people want to leave to "experts" the study of God and His relationship to the world, but this doesn't seem to be God's plan—at least not for our generation. Jesus said, "From everyone who has been given much, much will be demanded; and from the one who has been entrusted with much, much more will be asked" (Luke 12:48). We often think of "much" as referring to financial resources and material possessions, and so we give cash to churches and charities. But that's not what Jesus was talking about. He was talking about *knowledge*—the servant's knowledge of the master's will to be more specific. In other words, if we know what's expected of us and don't do it, we're more guilty than those who are ignorant.

Who knows more about God's expectations than our generation? Who has been given more knowledge, more revelation (Creation, Christ, and the complete text of Scripture), and more teaching than people alive today? Who has more copies of Scripture, more Bible study tools, more opportunities to learn about God than people living today in the United States?

Theology is for all of us, not just "the professionals," because God is revealing Himself to everyone, not just a few. What we believe about God affects our marriages, our families, our work, and everything we're involved in.

The writings of the prophet Jeremiah indicate why it's so important for everyone, not just professional clergy, to know God. The religious "experts" in Jeremiah's day were misrepresenting God by prophesying "the delusions of their own minds" (Jeremiah 23:26). They were leading people astray with "their reckless lies" (v. 32). Due to their dishonesty, the people did not know the true nature of God—that He "exercises kindness, justice and righteousness on the earth" (9:24).

I wonder if the same thing is happening today. I'm concerned that some people who call themselves Christians are showing the world a picture of an angry, vengeful God who is looking for any reason to annihilate them rather than a kind and compassionate God who is earnestly trying to convince them to believe His Son and accept His forgiveness.

LEARNING ABOUT GOD FROM CREATION

On a recent vacation, Jay and I went to see the mountains of the Pacific Northwest. We arrived at Mt. Rainier late in the afternoon, and hurried into the park. On the way up the mountain we stopped at various lookouts and took pictures of what we thought was Mt. Rainier.

Upon reaching Paradise Lodge, however, I realized that I had been taking pictures of the wrong mountain. It was beautiful, but it wasn't the one we had come to see. Mt. Rainier was shrouded in clouds. I had to ask people to tell me where the mountain was. Then I had to trust that what they told me was true. I pointed my camera into the clouds and snapped a few pictures so I would have some evidence that I had been there.

The next day was even worse. Rain. I decided I'd better stop fussing about what I couldn't see and start enjoying what I could! After all, I was surrounded by one of my favorite color combinations—green and white. The soft greens of emerging deciduous trees highlighted the darker shades of the forest evergreens. Fog formed by evaporating snowfields hovered above the trees and swirled between them like ghosts reluctant to leave. In many places, the taller trees pierced the fragile fog with their pointed tops. Waterfalls created by melting glaciers cut jagged white lines from the undulating clouds to the forest floor. Green poked out from the remaining snow. At lower elevations some wildflowers bloomed. I was witnessing the awakening of the forest.

So what if the mountain wanted to hide?!

I didn't need to view the majesty of a mountain to witness the amazing work of God. His wonder is equally evident in tiny plants that survive harsh brutal winters because God properly equips them. If rock formations rising out of the earth reveal God's strength and grandeur, the emerging new life of plants and animals reveals His tenderness. Maybe that was the message I needed to receive from God. I would accept it with gratitude. Even if I didn't see the top of the mountain, I had seen enough to remind me that creation is a stunning work of revelation and a jubilant call to worship.

On our third day at the foot of Mt. Rainier, we awoke to a hazy blue sky. *Could it be?* We packed our suitcases, ate our breakfast, loaded the car, and still the sun was out. But was the mountain? We drove into the park one more time.

At every turn of the winding road we looked up through the trees, up to the top of every glacier-filled crevasse. Not far into the park, I saw my first glimpse of Mt. Rainier's glory. Jagged lines of black granite rose in brilliant contrast to the white snow and blue sky.

Higher than any of the huge peaks around it—7,500 feet higher than the mountain I thought was "it"—Mt. Rainier was indeed the reigning king of mountain peaks.

There was no uncertainty once I saw it. I felt foolish for having been deceived by such a short imposter. Rainier was high and dangerous, but bright and beautiful.

As we stood at its foot and gazed at its face, I thought of the passage in John's gospel about Jesus and the Samaritan woman. As a result of the woman's testimony about her encounter with Jesus, many believed. But they wanted to know more, so they urged Jesus to stay, which He did. Later they said to the woman, "We no longer believe just because of what you said; now we have heard for ourselves, and we know that this man really is the Savior of the world" (adapted from John 4:4-42).

Previously I believed people's testimony about the mountain, but now my personal experience made the truth real. I knew for sure that the witnesses who had seen it had been telling the truth.

In e-mails to friends back home, I had joked that if we never saw Mt. Rainier from below the clouds, maybe we could see it from above them when we flew home. With that thought in mind, I boarded the plane with my camera hanging around my neck.

As the plane rose toward the west and then circled to the east, I spotted the mountain rising above the cloud cover. I raised my camera and started taking pictures past the young woman in the window seat. She politely moved forward and backward so I could get the best angle, but she showed no interest in looking out the window.

"You must live around here," I said. "I take it that you've seen the mountain before."

"I can see it from my bedroom window," she said. "I've grown up with it."

I thanked her for letting me take pictures and then got

settled for the three-hour flight. I took my Bible from my carry-on case to catch up on some reading I had missed while searching for mountains.

"Do you study theology?" the young woman asked me.

"Not formally," I said, "but I'm a Christian, and I believe the Bible tells me what I need to know about God and the meaning of life and how to live, so I try to follow it, even though I fail a lot."

"I'm trying to find a religion," she said. "My father is Buddhist, so I'm interested in that, but my mother is Episcopalian. She just gave me a Bible, but it's so big I don't know where to start reading."

I showed her the book of John in the New Testament and explained that the four gospels all tell the story of Jesus' life, but that John is probably the best one to read first to get a basic understanding of Christianity.

She asked more questions, and I explained, as briefly and simply as I could, what makes Christianity different from other religions. I told her about Jesus, about His death and resurrection, and how we can have our sins forgiven because of what He did on our behalf.

Later, as I thought about our discussion, I wondered, *Was my explanation of Christianity like a boring discourse on the history of a mountain or like an artist's rendition of its beauty? Did I convey to her that Christianity is even more beautiful than Mt. Rainier and even more important to pursue? Did I communicate the beauty of my faith or just facts? Did I describe my faith as being not just true but also strong and magnificent? Did the picture I showed her make her curious enough to want to see more? Did my "postcard" explanation describe Jesus in a way that made her eager to see and experience Him for herself? Will she now seek to find the one true God with as much enthusiasm as I sought a vision of the real Mt. Rainier?*

I thought of the similarity between the two of us. Her familiarity with Mt. Rainier was like mine with Christianity. Having grown up with it in my background, I often take Christianity for granted, not realizing that many have never seen a clear view of it and are still looking into the clouds, hoping to see the real thing, yet often being deceived by inferior imposters.

Before we got off the plane, I handed the young woman a business card and invited her to contact me if she had any questions. Whenever I think of her, I pray that God will protect the few seeds I was able to sow, that He will enable them to survive the brutal climate of today's popular culture, and that they will grow into a thriving plant.

God has His reasons for not letting me see certain things. In the case of Mt. Rainier, He wanted me to see something more important than a mountain's grandeur.

He wanted me to see His lavish, reliable tenderness so that it would be fresh on my mind when He placed me next to a young woman who needed to hear about God's loving kindness and compassion for all who seek Him.

Creation holds innumerable lessons about God like this one. We just need eyes that can see.

> If we cannot see God in the commonalities that constitute daily life, we would not recognize Christ if he walked into the room and sat down beside us.
>
> Don C. Skinner

LEARNING ABOUT GOD FROM SCRIPTURE

After observing some all-too-public disagreements between Christian leaders, I joked with some friends that someone ought to write a book titled *If God Is Such a Great Parent Why Can't His Children Get Along?*

A short time later I was listening to an interview with

one of my favorite authors, Philip Yancey, when I heard Philip say, "I probably shouldn't say this on radio, but, if I had to summarize the story of the Old Testament, I would use this phrase: It was God learning how to be a parent."

Was that true? I wondered. Did God have to *learn* to be a parent? Did He not know what was good for the very beings He created?

Yes, the Old Testament shows a vibrant picture of an amazing God who, though He Himself remains changeless, willingly changes His methodology. But does He change methods because He's "learning" to be a parent? Could it be instead that God changes strategies so He can reach as many people as possible? Before the apostle Paul ever used the phrase, "I have become all things to all men so that by all possible means I might save some" (1 Corinthians 9:22), I think God did exactly that.

I wouldn't argue about this because the way God tells the story it does indeed sound as if He's learning. I suspect, however, that God portrays Himself this way because He's trying to communicate on a level we can understand. After all, God didn't wait until He sent Jesus to start lowering Himself. He's been doing it all along. After creating the earth God didn't vacate the premises. He stayed around to socialize with His creatures. Apparently He even enjoyed spending time with them.

As far as I know, Adam and Eve are the only two humans who didn't start life as children. Scripture indicates that God created them, shall we say, post-puberty. And from what we read in Genesis, God walked with the young couple as their friend, not as their creator, their ruler, or even as their Father.

But all that changed when Adam and Eve traded truth

for a lie. As soon as they tried to tip the balance of power in their favor, they fell right off the scale.

Since then God has been working to restore the relationship. As part of His strategy He seems to be sending the human race back to the part Adam and Eve skipped—childhood.

So instead of saying that the Old Testament is the story of God learning to be a parent, I would say that it's the story of humans learning to be children. Jesus said, "I tell you the truth, unless you change and become like little children, you will never enter the kingdom of heaven" (Matthew 18:3).

One of the most important things children learn as part of a family is how to get along. Jesus' cousin John said, "This is how we know who the children of God are and who the children of the devil are: Anyone who does not do what is right is not a child of God; nor is anyone who does not love his brother" (1 John 3:10). And, "If anyone says, 'I love God,' yet hates his brother, he is a liar. For anyone who does not love his brother, whom he has seen, cannot love God, whom he has not seen" (1 John 4:20).

So back to the original question, "If God is such a great parent why can't His children get along?" I suspect it's because we're all trying so hard to prove that *we are right*, and that "Daddy loves me best." It's the spiritual version of sibling rivalry, and it should have no place among Christians.

The central message of Scripture is summarized in these words of Jesus: "A new command I give you: Love one another. As I have loved you, so you must love one another. By this all men will know that you are my disciples, if you love one another" (John 13:34-35).

Learning about God from Jesus

After a leisurely dinner at one of our favorite restaurants, a walk on the pier out to the lighthouse, followed by coffee at a local coffee shop, my husband and I and a friend headed home. Feeling relaxed from the exercise, invigorated by the conversation, and a bit high from the caffeine, I began telling a story.

When I was young, our family often went to the shoreline of Lake Michigan for a picnic during the warm summer months. On the way to the beach stood a home that we called "the messy house." Every time we passed it, both coming and going, someone would yell, "Drive slow, Dad, so we can see the messy house."

In all the times we drove past, we always saw the ironing board set up in the middle of the living room, and it was always heaped with clothes and surrounded by

49

piles of papers and magazines, boxes, toys, tools, and an assortment of dishes.

The messy house was one of the wonders of my young life. What seems odd to me now, however, is not how messy it was but how visible it was. Whatever time of the day or night we drove past, the drapes were wide open, and in the evening the lights were on. Not only did the family live in chaos; they didn't even try to hide it.

The story ended there, but I didn't have the sense to stop talking. "I still like it when people leave their drapes open and the lights on so I can see inside their houses," I added, my nose pressed against the car window as we drove through a residential area.

"What do you like about it?" our friend asked.

"I like knowing that other people are as messy as I am."

"And why is that?" he probed.

"It makes me feel better about myself."

"Why does that make you feel better?"

"Because at least I keep the drapes pulled so no one can see my mess," I blurted.

As soon as the words were out of my mouth, I knew that I had unintentionally jerked open the draperies that hid my own messy life.

I stopped talking then, but it was too late. Without a moment's hesitation our friend flicked a switch that flooded the scene with light.

"I guess that means you like seeing other people's messy lives but you're not willing to let them see yours," he said.

For a moment the light blinded me, but soon I saw what I had tried to hide: Vulnerability is something I recommend for others but reject for myself.

Ironically, I was once complimented for making myself vulnerable in my writing. I thanked the person, but I was really thinking, *This isn't true vulnerability. I'm not really making myself vulnerable. I'm simply trying to make myself acceptable by giving my character flaws a pleasing personality and making them entertaining. My self-disclosure has more to do with exhibitionism than true vulnerability.*

Self-exposure, of course, is the beginning of confession, but confession that stops at exposure has nothing to do with virtue. If it did, all the people who tell their perverted stories to talk-show hosts would be candidates for sainthood. Today's talk shows are a counterfeit confessional. People seem to think that by exposing their perversions they'll find acceptance when what they really need is redemption.

Confessing sin to gain acceptance for it falls far short of

the idea expressed in James 5:16: "Therefore confess your sins to each other and pray for each other so that you may be healed." True confession does not cause people to chuckle at sin; it causes them to weep. And the motive behind true confession is not a desire for admiration; it's a longing to be healed.

When we stop trying to make ourselves look good to others we have the opportunity to learn about true vulnerability. Vulnerability is *not* whitewashing our lives with religious activities and self-imposed rules which allow us to rationalize that we have no need for accountability. Vulnerability is acknowledging to ourselves and admitting to others our areas of weakness so that they can watch for signs of waywardness and gently nudge us back on track before we plunge into the abyss of serious sin with devastating consequences.

God exhibited the highest form of vulnerability when He dressed His Son in the thin skin of humanity and made Him the most vulnerable of all people: an infant. Christ was the embodiment of vulnerability because He was "susceptible to being wounded or hurt; open to criticism or temptation; open to attack or assault."

When I get the courage to try being vulnerable, I look for someone who loves me and will not use my secrets to hurt me. But God made Himself vulnerable to those who hated Him, who would ridicule His goodness, reject His love, and eventually kill Him.

The baby in the manger did not come to win a popularity contest; He came to win our redemption by allowing Himself to be hurt so that we could be healed. He didn't come to gain acceptance for Himself before the world; He came to gain acceptance for us before God.

Believing in God's Son

The way some people talk, you could get the idea that faith is nothing more than a spiritualized form of wishful thinking. "Just Believe" is a popular slogan that decorates everything from sweatshirts to wall hangings to Christmas cards and ornaments. But the kind of faith these advocate has more to do with the mystical power of positive thinking than anything God ever said on the subject.

Although it's silly to talk back to a slogan, someone ought to ask, "Believe what?" Believe that God will repay money we foolishly borrow? Believe that God will neutralize the consequences of our bad choices? Believe that God will give us the car, career, or spouse of our dreams if we promise to behave in a certain way?

Contrary to what we want to believe, faith is not convincing ourselves that we have God's stamp of approval on our plans; it's believing that God's plans are better than ours.

That's what Noah believed, and so at God's instruction he set about building a houseboat to save himself, his family, and a remnant of the animal kingdom from the flood God said was coming, even though Noah had no idea what was coming because he'd never in his life seen rain.

That's what Abraham believed, and so at God's command he left the comfort and familiarity of home and headed across the desert for a place God said was better, even though Abraham had never seen it.

That's what Moses believed, and so by faith he refused the privileges rightfully his as the son of Egypt's ruler and identified himself instead with people God said He had chosen for Himself, even though they were still slaves belonging to Pharaoh.

Biblical faith is not about taking risks; it's about taking on the identity of Jesus. It's not about having the audacity to do something risky; it's about having the courage to do what is right. It's not about running in the dark; it's about walking in the light. It's not about believing what people say about God; it's believing what God says.

The gospel of John uses the word *believe* more than any other book in the Bible. In fact, John claims to have been sent from God as a witness to testify so that all may believe (1:7).

Later John quoted Jesus: "The work of God is to believe in the one he has sent" (6:29). Belief is generally not thought of as work, but it is. Belief doesn't pour out of heaven and into our heads; it requires mental effort.

But people want God to do all the work. Even those who lived near Jesus and witnessed His miracles asked for more "proof." Comparing Jesus to Moses, they asked, "What miraculous sign then will you give that we may see it and believe you? . . . Our forefathers ate the manna in the desert; as it is written, 'He gave them bread from heaven to eat'" (John 6:30-31).

The startling thing about the request is that just the day before Jesus had indeed given them bread. He had fed five thousand of them with the bread from one boy's lunch!

Resisting the urge to say, "What about the bread I fed you yesterday!?" Jesus said instead, "I am the bread of life."

The reasons people give for not believing God often boil down to something they want God to do to prove Himself. Comedian Woody Allen has been quoted as saying, "If only God would give me some clear sign! Like making a large deposit in my name at a Swiss bank."

In making personal "to do" lists for God, we miss

seeing the countless things He has already done. When we wait in doubt and disappointment for God to do the one thing we demand of Him, we miss seeing everything God is doing and has already done.

Beyond Belief

Whenever I hear the song "God Is on Our Side," I feel uneasy. I think of some of the dastardly things that have been done by people boldly making this claim, and I fear that some people today are making it without the serious self-examination that must precede such a declaration. For God is only on the side of those who are on His side— those who desire to know His mind and do His will—not those who insist on convincing God that their way of doing things is right.

Abraham Lincoln said, "I do not boast that God is on

my side, I humbly pray that I am on God's side." Lincoln was expressing the idea set forth by Azariah to King Asa of Judah. After the Spirit of God came upon him, Azariah said, "The LORD is with you while you are with him. If you seek him, he will be found by you; but if you forsake him, he will forsake you" (2 Chronicles 15:2).

A friend once asked me, "Do you think Judas knew that he was wrong?" Well, I don't know, but I doubt it. Some of history's most despotic acts have been done by people convinced that their actions would make the world a better place. Many have even been done by those claiming to know God and be acting on His behalf. We should tremble at history's tragic lessons of those who believed with all of their heart that they were right when they were not.

One of my favorite Peanuts comic strips features

Charlie Brown saying to Snoopy, "I hear you're writing a book on theology. I hope you have a good title." Snoopy responds, "I have the perfect title: *Has It Ever Occurred to You That You Might Be Wrong?*"

Snoopy's question reminds us that no one is always right, and Paul's teaching reminds us that when we're wrong we need to "repent, turn to God, and do works befitting repentance" (Acts 26:20 NKJV).

The Greek word translated repent is *metanoia*, which means "change your mind." As Paul indicates, however, it does not mean just turning our heads toward God, nodding in polite agreement, and continuing on our own way. When we turn

A spinning coin cannot spin forever, nor can our minds remain undecided forever, since not to decide is itself a decision. . . . Either we conform our desires to the truth, or we conform the truth to our desires.

Os Guinness

our thoughts toward God—when we truly agree with Him about what is good—our behavior will follow. Like a car, we go in the direction we're pointed.

I once had a picture come to mind that helped me understand my faulty way of seeing spiritual things. I was thinking about the way the world is and the way Satan wants me to see it. I began imagining myself in a small, slow-moving picture. My back was to the camera, and in front of me were prison bars from one edge of the frame to the other—left to right and top to bottom. My hands were grasping the bars, and my face was pressed between them. Beyond the bars was a beautiful field with lots of lush grass, a bubbling brook with a waterfall, and beautiful flowering trees and plants that waved slightly in a soft, warm breeze. But the bars kept me from enjoying any of it. I could only long for what I had no way of reaching. I would occasionally shake the bars or bang my head against them, but it was all a self-defeating attempt to get what I believed I could never have.

As I watched, the perspective started changing. Little by little the camera moved back, showing me more of the picture. At first I was startled to see the wide-open space behind me. But as the camera moved back further, I was even more startled to see that what was behind me was the beautiful place I was longing for. In front of me—beyond the bars—was only a mirror reflecting it. As the camera moved back it also moved up, allowing me to see behind the mirror. And there was Satan, watching me through the one-way mirror, laughing because I had wasted so much time longing for his illusion. He knew all along that to get the real thing, all I had to do was turn around.

When we set our minds on things above we begin

to see the world as God sees it, and we see people as God sees them. We also come to know a God who is compassionate and gracious, slow to anger, and abounding in love and faithfulness (Exodus 34:6). And one day we'll be able to boast that we understand and know the LORD who exercises kindness, justice and righteousness on earth (Jeremiah 9:23-24).